meta morph o, sis

EVELYN CARREE

META MORPH O, SIS

Copyright © 2019 by Evelyn Carree

Dedication

To those seeking to understand sexual violence, may you go with an ear to listen and a heart to feel. Seek empathy, seek love.

To those who have loved me, even when I couldn't love you back, you are appreciated.

To secondhand survivors, your story matters too.

To the voices of the silent, my soul is receptive to your cries.

To those being suffocated by darkness in this very moment, this is a reminder to you that darkness has a time limit; it will not last forever. Seek moments of light, and try to expand them. They may be minute, they may be rare, but when a window of opportunity comes, focus on that light. Your focus will lead to expansion and conversion—Resurrection if you will. May you go with peace, love, and triumph.

Table of Contents

Introduction:

You are here. Come and see.

You are here for a particular reason, one I cannot define for you. Your soul has been carried to these pages, for a purpose far greater than you may be able to discern in this moment. I encourage you to move forward with a receptive heart. I am inviting you to **come and see** the depths of my being during a transformational process I now deem to be my Metamorphosis.

My Metamorphosis.

This evolutionary process is normally associated with a caterpillar that consumes food until the day it crystallizes into a cocoon. Within the cocoon, the caterpillar begins to morph. Only when this transformation is complete does the cocoon crack and reveal a beautiful butterfly. I found myself once as a caterpillar, feeding upon various experiences from an abusive relationship. I was full of many emotions that I was unable to process, up until the point of my crystallization. Here I was forced to accept and understand what I experienced. In the process, many truths came into my realm of consciousness. I *discovered the soul that was living within me* that had been suffocated by my ego. Through experience and personal revelation, I was able to grow into a new being and crack the cocoon I felt trapped in. *I grew my wings and someone more enlightened was brought into existence*. However, I was still shy to an extent. I was still afraid of this new body, this new "me" that had emerged. I had to find a new flow because *I knew I was never going to move the same again*. I struggled to feel confident enough to test out my wings to fly; I was intimidated by how high and *how far I could actually go if I just gave myself a chance. Only in my willingness to **lean into courage**, was I able to finally soar. Today I understand suffering differently. I appreciate each moment of my life, for I know that **each one** accumulates into **a greater purpose, a greater me.***

CONTENT WARNING: THIS BOOK IS ABOUT SEXUAL VIOLENCE, SPECIFICALLY RAPE. I WILL DISCUSS THE PROCESS OF TRAUMA AND HEALING.

meta-, *prefix*

denoting change, transformation.

meta • morph • o, sis

~the-punish-her
trapped in this closet
you block my only exit.
tears claw down my cheeks
burning words onto my face.
remember this day.

there was a silence
above my head.
a hollow hole
in the shape of your fist.

i felt the wall behind
my back support me
in more ways than one.

i felt its hugging presence
comforting me.
i've had a long day too.

i assert myself upwards.
trying to escape was pointless.
you dismiss me when i try.

readjusting on the floor
once again
i accept my defeat
in this moment.
my back to the wall
i lean in for a hug.
i close my eyes gently...
one day you will be free.

~the-confine-her
my feet rested upon the
glass of your windshield.
my toe prints presented
themselves boldly.
a position i have known to
calm me during our
parked car conversations...
you were emotional this night.
you made claims of desperation
i was unmoved.
you were compelled to
move me.
you accelerated the gas.
my back slammed against the seat.
recklessly we go down
each neighborhood street.
you wouldn't let me out
until we worked things out.
i begged you to stop.
your stubbornness took the wheel.
my stubbornness took the door
ready to exit the hard way.
you came to a calmness
and urged me to stay.
the car's velocity decreased
a mirror to your breath.
i followed your words
im sorry. pleasssse dont leave me...
each syllable pierced my ears.
your anger returned.

meta • morph • o, sis

the thought of me leaving
triggered you once again.
your expression of frustration
has repeated itself...
i look up to see shattered glass
through the footprints i had left.

~the-threaten-her
you felt the end of us
meant the end of you.

     ...

i hear clanking in the kitchen.
there is a shuffling in
the knife drawer.
i peer over to you
gradually
from the bedroom door.
i see your hoodie tightly
clenched around your head.
your eyes press into the floor.
each step you make
stut-ttt-tt-ters
one after the other.
with a grasp on the knife
whispers of *"let me do this"*
seep from your mouth
to taint the air around us.
i remove the knife from your fist.
you rush outside to escape from the
temptations you've left in the air.

~her
her copper skin shimmers
under the vault of heaven.
her charcoal braids
bounce with each s-k-i-p
along the mellow exterior
of mother earth.
filled with stories of harmony
about friendship to the land
she seeks to weave her essence
into the source of all nature
to live long after she is gone.
mixing the light from above
and the love from within
she molds a bed of
honey coated friends.
she names them *sunflowers.*
born of the sun
living through her love
in *the garden of eden.*

~the-outside-her
clothed in sunshine
with a smile at her center
echoing the hue of her creators.
rooted deeply
dancing effortlessly
she is surrounded by many of her sisters.
she peeks as footsteps approach from a far.
expanding her petals
breathing with the wind
sending a warm h e l l o.
the outsider's jaw
lowers in awe
his impulses rise.
dropping low into the dirt
he looks into her eye to eye.
the outsider wraps his
fingers around her base
removing her from her home.
unaware of the separation he's created.
he takes her as a token
that's what he understood to be "love".
after a few days time
she is weak and wilted.
he "loves" again and again
until he can no more.
the cycle he prolonged
is responsible for
the desolation
in the garden of eden.
she leaves nothing behind.

meta • morph • o, sis

~the-swim-her
my ocean flows heavenly
resting in the will of my palms.
though i flourish abundantly
every drop is known personally.

you seek me to nourish your famished soul.

dipping your toes
wiggling in quietly
you deepen your presence
until your whole body is
i m m e r s e d.
inebriated in my waters
the warmth slowly
leaves you in a state
of rapturous delight.

you left behind contaminating germs
which multiplied after your departure.

sunshine no longer visits.
the water has become chilled.
the waves splash differently now.
the waves splash differently now.

meta • morph • o, sis

~the-rob-her
if you keep your house unlocked
then you deserve to get robbed.

if you don't have a security system
you can't prove there was theft.
                   ...
if you wouldn't have people over
no one would know what
you have in your house.
                   ...
somehow there is always
an excuse for someone
to break the law and
take what was
n e v e r
theirs to have.

the robber is gone.
his aroma remains.
flashbacks of him are
imprinted into the floor.
his fingertips have
left stains in intangible places.
he's taken a p i e c e of me
my *peace* from me.

meta • morph • o, sis

~the-pollute-her
globally i am warming
overrun by c-o-2.
layers of
frustration
and
anger
are clustering under my pores.
the openings of my skin
have met interference.
my temperature rises
each day.

you polluted my world
desensitizing my nerves
ending in a need for
reprogramming.
you forced me to re-learn
basic functionality.
you left my body paralyzed.
i am still unable to exhale.

meta • morph • o, sis

~the-haunt-her
haunted daily.
you've become my shadow.
i tried to exfoliate you away.
tried to re-baptize myself for days.
tears have emerged in these waters.
they were supposed to cleanse me.

i am floating in scarlet.
a vampire's fondest fantasy.

~the-rock-her
i watch you rock
back and *forth*
you ask...
what's wrong with me...?

it happened so suddenly
i'm asking myself the same thing.
we've both been traumatized
by this person who has
emerged in your body
he has
s l o w l y
c r e p t
i n
showing himself
in glimpses.

this is not me
forgive me
i love you

more incidents.
more intensity.
more danger.
each *time* was a warning.
time knew all along
this day would come.

meta • morph • o, sis

~the-decide-her
amidst those
deciding your fate
i w i t h e r e d
away *slowly.*
i knew you
already decided
mine.

your future was bright.
my present was dim.
they willingly overlooked me
unwilling to send another
b l a c k   m a n
to the *system.*
they willingly
preserved you
while ignoring your
unwillingness to
preserve me.

~the-random-creep-her
i see your eyes
project your fantasies
as they tune in and
trickle down my legs
recording every inch
as if you'd be watching
me in your mind later.

i feel your eerie
steps disrupt the
steady vibration
of the floor
as you move
closer to me
for attention.

i smell the eagerness
on your breath as
your tongue circles
your lips ready to press
them into my skin.

i show no interest
you think im
playing hard to get.

really the message
i'm sending isn't
hard to get
i'm just *not* into y o u.

meta • morph • o, sis

~the-random-lust-her
your eyes fondle
my hair like a
deck of cards
sucking away
my holiness
in an instant.

burying your focus
in my chest
you stare deeper
when i'm resistant

as if my
disapproval
was enough to
trump your
persistence.

meta • morph • o, sis

~her panic
the weight of the world
on top of me
i can hardly breathe.

collapsing in hysteria
eyes an endless ocean
i can hardly see.

a state of electrocution
filled with lightning bolts
new openings burst.

energy is desperate to vanish
hoping this would release
all the shocks within.

eventually the bolts
dismiss themselves
leaving my flesh buzzed.

light has been sucked out of me.
i exist as a hollow space
a dark abyss.

just a simple thunderstorm now.

meta • morph • o, sis

~her fear
my amygdala is a siren
sending warnings to my body
letting me know
it might be a long day.

tension causes fever.
in this case
i'm sweating bullets
dropping bombs
on my future.

condensation.
evaporation
of every goal
i laid in front of me.

amygdala.
not friends with the
calming ocean that i know
resides within me.

so easily i'm afraid.
it's beginning to offend me.
someone send me foreign aid.

meta • morph • o, sis

~her cry
under pressure
her tears press her
she doesn't feel them
but they still fall.
seeing how things were
and how things are
slowly drown her deeper.

she's adapted to the flood
now a little mermaid.
her body moves with grace
carrying a mind that's unsaved.
swimming amongst old memories
nostalgia fills her eyes.
overwhelmed in her solitude
liquefied by her cries.

the only woman in atlantis
she's surrounded by coral reef.
both endangered.
both in danger.

~her emptiness
as a balloon
once high on helium
air escapes me
over time.
the only inclination
of my life
was my breath.
now so shallow
it's become impossible
to find.
things move in
s l o w - m o t i o n
yet swiftly motion moves.
obligations call my name
i drown them out
in my window pane.
i lay as nothingness.
a vacancy of sensation.
my rubber edges
e x p a n d . . .
hopelessly.
a silhouette
honoring a life
now lifeless.

~her matrix
back in this place
a haunted house 24/7
crawling with
shattered glass
and unknown corners.
pieces of my reflection
have me surrounded.
i'm in the center of
imposters.
who am i?
i am lost...
in a personalized matrix.

~her/e
i wanna sleep here.
i can't seem to escape.
might as well have a
slumber party with agony.

it's easy to stay here.
a pool of isolation
i can complain
even refrain
from all responsibilities.

it's cold here.
ice frosts my passion
yet creativity thrives.
somehow lack of fire
combined with torture
meshes into a desire.

i'm afraid here.
i fear that i may stay
though there's no way
for me to move forward
if i remain here.

can you hear?
the aching silence
that oddly has a sound.
trickles down your eardrum
and starts to compound
your heart - - your lungs

choking on the song
you could have sung
if you never came here.
but you did.
you *stayed here.*
you were meant to
pass through.
you were never
meant to *stay* here.

~her flower
my rose petals have faded
i am coarse to the touch.
an antagonist to beauty
i wither away as such.

no sunshine and roses
simply sunburns and thorns.
i am replaced by a soreness
my glow no longer forms.

~her mourning
if only i could be released
from the zombies in my bed.
they tie down my limbs
and shove stories in my head.

today was supposed to be new
i was going to explore.

the day is over.
i lay mute once more.

~her pick 6
each happy moment can be
intercepted
if darkness is around.
it awaits one
touch
to bring all hopes
down.
she treads her days lightly
taking no risks with what she has.
she holds her joy tightly
thinking that will make it last.
she receives false security
from the fear that she's trapped in.
not knowing this alone leaves her
a pick 6 waiting to happen.

~her tree
as the last leaf
of an autumn tree
cleaving to what's *dead*
for the memory.

the last leaf has fallen
it no longer lived
soaking with the other
leaves that once did.

morph, v.

to undergo transformation.

~the portraits
we started and finished
today with a portrait.
we explored the
portraits of the world.
many people
to be celebrated.
we ended the night
with me painting you
with you motivating me
to *paint myself*
to *stretch myself*
to scary places.

bold and necessary
was my exploration.

~the awakening
trials are an awakening of the soul.
they remind you of the inevitable
limitations that rest upon on your flesh.
we are *limited* in stature.
our infinite nature is only
possessed when
combined with our spirit
and connected to the
source of all creation.
only then can we
extend ourselves
past minds view.
only then can we
evolve into a nature
beyond our mortal state.

~the transformation
know that vessels
of healing flow
within you medicinally.
the very wounds carved
into you for your *annihilation*
are stitched and primed
with love for your
transformation.

meta • morph • o, sis

~the ego
the ego makes you
the center of the universe.
it confuses a difficult day
as a life of disfavor.

when we are led by the ego
we become its slave
living in a false identity
allowing space for pity
to exploit our divinity.

when we surrender ego
we allow our precious nature
to resonate and press through
sharing energy of delight
to all we come in contact with.

light extends to our neighbor.
love becomes inclusive.
all life truly becomes one.

~the root
moments of sorrow
bring an indulgence
of *physical pleasure.*
there's an idea that binging
on the external world
could replenish the hole
disguising itself as the stomach.

that gut wrenching feeling
is root of all chakras
the root of your being.
it is the inner corner of your soul
that's *hungering for you*
that's *starving* for affection.
feed this place *first.*
feed it with *the source.*
harvest on all the energy within
and you will **never hunger again.**

meta • morph • o, sis

~the earth
i came to know you
resonating deeply
with your wounds.
you've been exploited
just.like.me.
men have taken from us both
though they have taken
from you much longer.

i feel your soul, mother.
your vibrations have
been my *meditations.*
your warmth
my blanket of safety.
with each step i take
i know i am not alone.

~the woman
karma is a woman.
she seeks justice
providing cards to humanity
reading *"consequences."*

she provides us each a chance
to rise up and become
who we were destined to be.
karma is a woman.

meta • morph • o, sis

~the decision
a decision to isolate
an event to *specific emotions*
invites *particular perceptions*
of the world.

an effort to dedicate
a mood to a day
can be *liberating*
yet r.e.s.t.r.i.c.t.i.v.e.
life truly is what you make it.

~the opposition
to die is to
b l o o m
to wilt is to
g r o w

to understand
is to *listen.*
listen to the cries
each moment releases.
seek the bond that
cohesively combines
all which was lost
to all that can be restored.
unveil the intimacy
that exists in opposition.

~the eviction
light enters a room and says to the darkness
it's time for you to go.

meta • morph • o, sis

~the sun
the sun
i like the sun.
when she sets
to see her rise
to feel her heat
seeping past my eyes.
soaking into my skin
melanin drips
down my shoulders
to my feet.
the soles beneath
burn into the surface
of mother earth
in harmony with
her-heart-beat.

the sun
i like the sun.
when she lightens
the way
or provides warmth
from her rays
i raise a question...
where do you go?
why do you leave?

she says to me
i will return...
right now, there are others who need me.

meta • morph • o, sis

~the moon
through me
you'll understand
light will not always
come blaring in your face.
sometimes you must look
behind me to know
it is always there.

meta • morph • o, sis

~the mother
an ending is the *mother* to a new beginning.

meta • morph • o, sis

~the bees
each day comes with chaos.
you struggle to survive.
bees swarm your mind
as you imitate their hive.

you hold them hostage
as if you need them
when peace would fill you
if you freed them.

meta • morph • o, sis

~the vines
you can only *swing* to the vines ahead
if you *release* the vines from behind.

meta • morph • o, sis

~the old
i watch old pieces
of who i was fall away.
i question the separation.
when i'm fully exfoliated
caressing my smooth skin
i recognize the beauty
and appreciate the removal
of all that was
toxic.
dirty.
and
dead..

~the time
at *three* o'clock
shadows of you lay over me.
you taint my aura
leaving me to search
uncharted territory.
i'm playing hide and seek
with my conscious.
your dominion reigns over me.
it can only be penetrated by light.
increased composition of this energy
revealed all remnants of you.
bit-by-bit
i watch this cremation.
light is all that's left.
1..2..*three*...
beams of me surround you
graciously extending
effortlessly
channeling
forgiveness.
i seek to capture
every moment
wrapping it
concealing it
setting it free.
forgiveness is yours.
three..2..1...
it is done.

o, sis...

(O, brother.)

a phrase often used in admiration or
empowerment towards oneself or others.

meta • morph • o, sis

~a great breath of silence
rumor is
all things have a sound.
i could finally hear it.
the great breath of
s i l e n c e
synchronized with the
rhythm of my heart.
an opening was divulged.
it is in this space that
god's voice was magnified.
a resonation of peace
filled every *exhalation.*

meta • morph • o, sis

~the first of its kind
the first of everything
carries a sensation
flawlessly exclusive
the only one of its kind.

meta • morph • o, sis

~evolution
evolution is like
baking a cake.
you must stay
until the end
to *reap fully*
from the process.

meta • morph • o, sis

~each moment *is*
neither in nostalgia
nor anticipation
does happiness lie
but in the stillness
of each moment.

~i deserve this moment.
intimacy ceases to vacate
as time advances.
my soul reveals herself
unlatched and untied.
his words
t i p - t o e
down her spine
caressing her with
whispers of velvet.

is this love?

she neither claims nor denies
for she knows that either way
this is **but a moment**.

meta • morph • o, sis

~i deserve fond memories.
left with a paintbrush
and images of you.
moments are spent
inscribing our memories
shading the tune of your voice.

heeeey beautifullll.

as if theses strokes
could imitate the
strokes of your
hands through my hair.
my favorite meditation.

~i deserve intimacy.
fragrances float
as atoms in the atmosphere.
laced in the oxygen i inhale
oozing slowly
they flow through
e v e r y vessel
permeating my core.
i am enthralled
not a moment too soon.
deeply gazing into you
your tone offers
gentle vibrations of ecstacy.
my mind oscillates
in a low alpha state.
you remind me to
inhale
once again.

~i deserve devotion.
i lay in a bath
amongst roses
handpicked by you.
the incense you left
is integrated in them.
they enrapture my skin
seeping
into the inner
lining of my existence.
your presence is a present
one i couldn't have anticipated.
your endless devotion to loving me
circulates my emotions.
i feel unwined and connected.
inhaling once again
i see you are still with me
in every p e t a l you've left.

~i am thankful for my body.
i used to detach everything
that has happened to you, from me.
to acknowledge the wounds on you
i had to acknowledge
the carelessness of me.
at times i blamed myself for
everything you had to feel
and everything you had to heal from.
i am sorry.
i know that i never
physically harmed you
but i didn't know how
to protect you either.
i am sorry it took me
so long to get things right.
thank you for trusting me.
thank you for knowing that
one day i would turn your
wounds into stripes.
each stripe is a reminder
of your strength
not your weakness.
thank you for always loving me.
today, i love you too.
i love you because *you are.*

meta • morph • o, sis

~i am at home in my body
you carry me forwards
when my thoughts are weak.
you are the steps of courage
i am too fearful to take.
everywhere i adventure to
you are there with me.
you are delicately formed
the muse of my creativity.
you bring a stillness
through my breath.
you are my daily touch of peace.
you are the cradle to my spirit
the home of my soul.

meta • morph • o, sis

~i am unlimited potential.
your
special eyes
specialize
in loving me.
i was a particle of dust
dissipating in the sea.
by god's grace
you discovered me.

you are a reflection of
unlimited potential.
with you
access was granted
to tap into
every instance
every moment
using the totality of us to evolve.
indeed the vitality lies not
in the body alone
but in solidarity
with the spirit.

meta • morph • o, sis

~i am divinity
art and nature
we feel as one.
under the sun
simultaneously *soaking*
rays of intimacy
of *unity*
growing into our
divinity.
my joy is
skyrocketing into
infinity.

never felt so good to be free
never felt so good to be me.

~i am blessed.
blessed are they who see with the eyes of their soul.

meta • morph • o, sis

~i am a factory of love.
she traveled the world
to find herself
never thought
to plan a trip within.
just a few moments daily
could transfer her energy in.
all of the goodness has combined
developing a factory with
an endless production of love.

~i am a kiss from the sun.
she is the *beat* of the earth
the *breath* that is the wind.
she is the *sway* of the sea
the *energy* of the waves.
she is an accumulation of
kisses from the sun.

~i am tiger lily.
the lilies *grow freely*
intertwined with the spirit that
generously flows through the land.
energy is sent from the earth
resonating with *who they are.*
living with a deeper knowing
in the *present moment,* they are
liberated by their existence.
young. wild. *free.*

meta • morph • o, sis

~we are rays of heat.
soaked in warmth from above
a transmission begins to
move from the *external* world to
the *internal* realms of my body.
my spirit begins to radiate
towards those in my proximity.
others receive and begin
to radiate themselves.
love is merely a conduction of heat.

meta • morph • o, sis

~we are conquerors.
my greatest triumph
is living through
lifeless days and
daunting nights
to tell you that
you. are. a. conqueror.

~we are sunshine.
my sun will provide you
with warmth until you
can connect and become your
own sunshine.

meta • morph • o, sis

~we are the echo.
if i only focus on the
difficulty of my steps
i'll fail to look up and
see the angels that are near
and the troubled souls behind me.
their pleas fill my heart.
claim victory for **us.**

when i speak
and you hear an echo
know that it's because
I am not alone.

~you deserve unison.
you *deserve* to find
someone in unison
with the wavelengths
you emit.

meta • morph • o, sis

~you are autonomous over your body
this is your home.
choose the aromas
that flow through the air
and the paintings
upon the wall.
play your favorite music
dance in your pajamas
or sit and do nothing at all.
cook if you want
or be cooked for.
invite people in
if you choose to.
allow them to stay
as long as you see fit.
this is your *home*.
this is *your* home.

meta • morph • o, sis

~you are unlimited potential.
placing limits on
your divinity
is like trying to
see and describe
a color outside of
the visual spectrum.
you just can't do it.

meta • morph • o, sis

~you are present in this moment.
tune into the energy
carried by your words
and your presence.
notice the movement
through your body.
feel the lightness
of your breath.
experience the
stillness of your mind.
notice the person you
become when you
acknowledge yourself.

~you are divinity.
you are composed of precious layers
simply to be revered and recognized.
you have intrinsic value
given to you by your creator
it cannot be altered nor taken away.

this is d i v i n i t y.

this is your nature in its *purest* form.
we can invite reverence
towards ourselves and others
with a smile of love.

meta • morph • o, sis

~you are a star.
you are surrounded
by space above.
the tints of midnight
accentuate your features.
the darker it becomes
the brighter you shine.
thank you for being a star in the sky.

meta • morph • o, sis

~you are handcrafted.
god *spoke* the world into existence
but *handcrafted you*.

meta • morph • o, sis

~you are drawn perfectly.
you are caught into an illusion
that being drawn to him
is a reflection of what
he can draw to you.

when really
he simply draws from you.
he takes a piece from you
leaving you only to see
the pieces he didn't want.
leaving you to draw conclusions
that you are incomplete without him.
when really
you are incomplete with him.

you were drawn perfectly all this time.

meta • morph • o, sis

~you are art.
look at yourself
through the lens
of your creator
and *you will* see
a work of art.

meta • morph • o, sis

~you are free.
embrace your experiences
they have given you wings.
at moments you will struggle
remember *this is not who you are.*

one day you will notice
things feel natural.
you will be free.
free to fly
fly away to more.
more life.
more you.
a greater purpose
awaits you.
fly, fly, away.

A message for all:

I am not just speaking to the heterosexual woman who has been sexually violated by a man. I am not just speaking to survivors of sexual violence. I speak to you all. Indeed we are **ALL** impacted by sexual violence. We all must acknowledge our deepest connection to one another. ***When part of the world hurts***, in one way or another, ***the rest of the world hurts***. It's not enough to only pay attention to an issue when it directly impacts you, because painfully, you never know when it might strike you or someone you love. God forbid that moment comes, but if it did, you may find yourself seeking help from others who, like the "old you," are unwilling to "get involved." This is not just an ordinary issue, it is a **human rights** issue. Sexual violence does not discriminate. People ***everywhere,*** regardless of any identifier you can associate with a person, ***suffer from sexual violence***. It is important to remember this so that we can be inclusive when we offer love and support to survivors.

A message to survivors:

Thank you for joining me today. I know that your journey through these pages may have been challenging. I understand that you may feel stuck, eagerly searching for a way out. I know that you may feel unsure about your value, your purpose, and even how much longer you can live on this earth. Remember that you are overcoming a traumatic experience that you did not deserve. However, since you are experiencing it, I encourage you to continue fighting. Your journey will transform your life into something more beautiful than before *if you allow it to.* This can be done by loving yourself through whatever state you pass through.

You were never meant to do this alone.
You may experience moments of loneliness. These moments will consume you and begin to convince you that you are the only one feeling how you do. These moments will make you feel like no one cares about you or the pain you are feeling. You may even believe that no one understands you. This is not true, nor will it ever be. Many people are suffering, just like you are. This is not an experience that you have to overcome by yourself. *No one was meant to heal on their own.*

Your journey is not in vain.

Healing is cyclical and unpredictable at times. One evening you may feel like breaking, the next morning the weight of the world has been removed. You may be wondering, *why me?* I can't specifically tell you *why,* but I have a prediction. You are experiencing this journey because *you* have an enduring spirit. You were built with the strength to overcome. An introduction to a traumatic misfortune like this should reemphasize to you *just* how powerful your nature is. Remember that your journey will continue to strengthen you as you press forward. Remember that you are surrounded by others on similar journeys to evolution. You may be a caterpillar searching for food, or a butterfly struggling to activate your new set of wings. Wherever you may be, remember that people are watching you. You may be blessed to bless another through a situation you have overcome. You may find that someone else is able to inspire *you* to stay on the path of evolution. Every journey is unique, and every journey is *powerful. No journey is in vain.*

Express yourself.

You don't have to be trapped by powerful emotions. Your story is **yours.** Your expression is **yours.** When you are ready, seek a healthy way to express what you feel. Use your emotions as fuel for this avenue of expression. Set the hauntings free.

The day before

Each day serves the days that have yet to come. For something to rise, it must reside in a lower state first. The *day before* is the lower state. Without the lower state, there would be a flatness to life, preventing all pain and all joy, removing the law of opposition from existence.

The day before Jesus Christ rose from the dead, there was darkness and sorrow for many. The day before your resurrection may be just the same. Remember that moments of darkness have prepared you to elevate into a new state of life. When you struggle to find hope, remember *that day* is simply **just the day before.**

Remember, remember:

You're entitled to ***feel your pain*** how you want to feel it. Allow your experiences to serve you. Express who ***you*** are, how ***you*** want. Find safe spaces and ***seek comfort there***. Move into your evolution ***without judgment***. Increase your faith in the unseen. Remember that your ***healing is within***, and will always be an ***infinite energy of love***. Let others love you, and let yourself ***love others***. Be who you are boldly, fiercely, and intentionally. ***Have courage*** in the places you've been and the places you will be. ***Take steps forward***, even if you take them slowly. No matter where you go, or who you may see, ***remember, remember, who you are.***

With light and love,
Evelyn Carree ~ Evey ~ Tiger Lily

About the Author

Evelyn Carree was born and raised in Arlington, Texas. After high school, she left to attend Texas A&M University for college. During her sophomore year of college, she became a statistic; she became one of the many individuals raped in college.

Though her rapist did not attend Texas A&M, he still tainted the city. Graduating from college began to slowly fade away as a distant desire, her focus was simply graduating from her trauma each day.

This experience shortly became a source of inspiration for her. instinctually, she leaned into her place of comfort: *artistic expression.* She took her feelings of discombobulation to the pages of her journal to unravel the unique feelings she was experiencing. Writing offered her freedom that was unknown off the page.

During this time, she began to notice the intrinsic value of nature; it became her primary source of connection and love. In this place of connection, there was a mutual understanding of what it meant *to be acted upon.*

This is where she and God met to explore the realms of all possibilities within her and in the world. The oneness she feels through God in nature inspires many of her artistic pieces today.

Purpose Gang Publishing

x

Book Launch On Demand

www.ingramcontent.com/pod-product-compliance
Lightning Source LLC
Chambersburg PA
CBHW051735040426
42447CB00008B/1151